Your Social Security Retirement Toolkit

A Step-By-Step Guide to Getting the Money, Benefits & Financial Support *You Are Entitled to in Your Golden Years*

By Dr. Donna Davis

Your Social Security Retirement Toolkit
Copyright © 2017 by Donna Davis.

ISBN: 10: 0692824103
ISBN: 13: 978-0692824108

Publisher's Note: The author and publisher have made every effort to ensure that the information in this book was correct at press time. The author and publisher do not assume and hereby disclaim any liability to any party for any loss, damage, or disruption by errors or omissions, whether such errors or omissions result from negligence, accident, or any other cause. Further, the author or publisher does not have any control over and does not assume responsibility for author or third-party websites or their content. This book is not intended as a substitute for medical advice of physicians or other trained medical professionals.

First Printing 2017
Golden Goddess Press
PO Box 6928
Snowmass Village, CO 81615
www.boomerblasts.com

Old age is at once the most certain, and for many people the most tragic of all hazards. There is no tragedy in growing old, but there is tragedy in growing old without means of support.

— Franklin Delano Roosevelt

Introduction

At 58, I didn't know when I could apply for Social Security, how much my payments would be, or what Medicare covered.

The truth is I never wanted to know. Retirement seemed so far off, but now, the fear of my financial future was overcoming my desire to avoid the inevitable.

Retirement was coming, and it was time to prepare. I spent months devouring books, articles, websites, government pamphlets, and more. It was daunting. I read before work, at lunch, at night, and on the weekends. There was an enormous amount of information, but I was determined to plow through.

In the end, I felt confident I could make good decisions and not fall victim to misinformation and common mistakes. That is why I chose to create a guide on retirement, something I wished I had throughout this entire process.

To make it easier for you, I condensed hundreds of pages of information into one concise package using simple everyday language.

In this book, you will:

- Gain insight into the Social Security Program

- Understand your choices

- Obtain the confidence to take charge of your benefits

- Have the courage to question information because you know what's right

- Avoid mistakes

- Get the benefits you deserve

Nearly half of all baby boomers are not financially prepared for retirement, which makes it critical that you get everything that's yours. Knowing the facts will save you time, save you money, and give you peace of mind.

This book will enable you to take charge of your benefits so that you can make the right decisions and create a better future for you and your family.

Get your copy of

The Ultimate Social Security Retirement Cheat Sheet

at: www.boomerblasts.com

Table of Contents

Why Social Security?..9
Social Security: SSA, SSI, DI,
What Is the Difference? 13
Who Pays? 19
Who Gets Paid? Are You Eligible? 21
Full Retirement Age:
What's that? 25
Should You Apply at 62?..27
How Long Do You Need to Provide for Yourself? 31
How is your Benefit Amount Determined? 35
Can You Work and Collect Social Security? 39
Is Social Security Taxed?...43
What if You Are Married? 47
What if I'm Divorced?..53
Are Same Sex-Couples Eligible
for Social Security Benefits? 57
What If My Spouse Has Died? 59
Windfall Elimination Provision (WEP) 63
Government Pension Offset (GPO).............................67
How Can You Apply? 69
Can You Collect Social Security
While Living Abroad?..73
Social Security and Women 79
What is the Best Time to Begin Collecting
Social Security? 85

PART 2
Changes Due to The Bipartisan Budget Act of 2015

The File and Suspend 89
The Restricted Application...91
The Claim and Switch 93
Conclusion 95

Bonus Section
MEDICARE

Eligibility..1
Part A 5
Part B...11
Part C 15
Part D 17
Medigap 21
Conclusion 25

References...i
Acknowledgements vi
About the Author viii

Chapter 1

Why Social Security?

Social Security is the national insurance program of the United States. It provides income to older and disabled workers. It insures that U.S. citizens and legal residents who have worked in our country have income later in life or if they become disabled.

In order to be eligible for Social Security Retirement or Disability Insurance, you must be a citizen or legal resident. You or an eligible family member must have worked in the United States for a minimum of 10 years. Illegal residents do not qualify for or receive Social Security Retirement or Disability benefits.

The Social Security Act was passed into law in 1935. It provided benefits to retirees aged 65 or older. Its purpose was to help pay for the basic necessities of life – food, clothing, and shelter – to those who qualified. Benefits for disabled workers were added later.

Social Security is the most successful program ever instituted by the American government. It raised the standard of living of millions of Americans and lifted many out of poverty.

Prior to Social Security as our citizens aged and could no longer work, they were unable to support themselves. Most had not earned enough to be able to save for retirement. (That was a luxury reserved for the privileged.) The result was that if retirees had no family, church, or other charitable institution to provide for them, as many didn't, they may have ended up homeless, starving, and without medical care. Many of the destitute ended up in a poorhouse, which were institutions that often-provided substandard living conditions. Many of the elderly suffered untimely and undignified deaths.

The elderly population grew dramatically in the early 1900s as health care, public sanitation, and better living conditions enhanced American life. It was the Great Depression from 1929 to 1939 that exposed the vulnerability of all but the very wealthy and led to the start of Social Security.

It's Great for the Economy

You may hear that Social Security is a drain on the federal budget and our economy. Nothing could be further than the truth. Social Security fuels our economy. In 2015, the Social Security Administration distributed over $870 billion to more than 59 million people. Most of that goes back into our economy in payments to landlords, grocery stores, clothing outlets, gas stations, utilities, etc. The funds provide jobs coast to coast.

Many claim that undocumented workers deplete Social Security funds. The truth is that illegal immigrants and their employers contributed $13 billion in payroll taxes to Social Security in 2010 that they can never claim. Undocumented immigrants contribute exponentially more to Social Security than they can ever receive.

There is a lot of confusion about the basic rules and regulations of Social Security. This can cause you to make decisions that are not the best for you. You may have tried to navigate government websites, or read books and articles, yet you come away baffled. This book will clear up some of the misconceptions and make the procedures easy to understand and accessible to all.

Knowing the primary policies will give you a strong foundation for making good decisions. Your choices are critical and will affect you and your family members permanently. This book will help you get the financial support you are entitled to over your lifetime.

Steps to be eligible:

- You must be a U.S. citizen, legal resident, or eligible family member to collect Social Security.

- You must be between the ages of 62 and 70 to apply for retirement benefits.

- You need a total of 40 credits. You earn one credit for each $1,300 earned with a maximum of four credits per year.

- You must have worked a minimum of 10 years and earned at least $5,200 (2017) in each of those years to obtain 40 credits.

If you worked for the railroad, there is a separate government agency that administers your retirement benefits, the Railroad Retirement Board. The RRB is an independent federal agency responsible for providing benefits to eligible employees of the railroad industry and their families. Social Security and the Railroad Retirement Program have many similarities but there are still major differences in structure and funding between the two. If you are eligible for benefits from the RRB, please contact the board directly at www.secure.rrb.gov for specific information on your coverage.

Chapter **2**

Social Security: SSA, SSI, DI, What Is the Difference?

Trying to make sense of the different government programs available to retirees can be challenging. In this chapter we look at what each one covers, clarify the purpose of the programs, and see who is eligible.

SSA or the Social Security Administration is a U.S. government agency that provides income to retirees, survivors, and the disabled that have worked. Each division provides a particular service and has different eligibility requirements.

Social Security is funded mainly by payroll tax. You contribute 6.2% of your earnings, and your employer matches that, for a total of 12.4% paid on your behalf. Once collected, the tax is divided between two Social Security Funds: the OASI and DI.

OASI, Old Age and Survivor's Insurance, is the retirement and survivor portion of Social Security. It currently receives 3.83% of the payroll tax collected.

DI, Disability Insurance, also known as SSDI, may cover qualified workers and their families in the event one becomes disabled. Not all disabled individuals are eligible for DI.

You must meet basic *Social Security* eligibility requirements and specific medical criteria. The Disability Insurance Fund receives 2.37% of the payroll tax.

To be eligible for Social Security Retirement or Disability benefits:

- You must have earned 40 credits during your work career. You receive one credit for every $1,300 earned with a maximum of four credits per year. Generally, you must have earned four credits per year for at least 10 years to receive benefits.

- For OASI, you must be at least 62 years of age. For survivor benefits, you must be at least 60 years old (widow or widower). There is no age requirement for Disability Insurance, but you must have a qualifying disability.

Social Security payment amounts are based on earned income. The higher your earnings, the higher your monthly payment will be until the maximum, which is $2,687 at Full Retirement Age. Working off the books or not paying tax on your full income when self-employed, can lead to a diminished monthly payment.

Full Retirement Age used to be 65 but now depends on the year you were born. If you were born 1943-1954, your Full Retirement Age is 66. For those born 1955 -1960, the Full Retirement Age will gradually increase to 67.

The maximum income taxed in 2017 is $127,200. After that amount, neither you nor your employer pay Social Security tax on additional income.

If you are collecting disability from Social Security, once you reach your Full Retirement Age, you will be switched from disability to retirement benefits. The payment amount will stay the same as the two are calculated with the same formula.

As a worker, if you have not contributed enough to Social Security to earn 40 credits, you will not qualify for retirement benefits. If you are disabled though, the number of credits needed may be less.

Social Security is based on your lifetime earnings – not on your current income – and the age you decide to retire.

Some examples of what you can expect:

If you are currently 60 and earned an average of $50,000 per year over your working life, you would get about $1,822 per month if you decided to retire after you turn 62. That amount would increase to

$2,470 per month if you retire after the age of 66. If you wait until age 70 to retire, the monthly amount would increase to $3,195.

Social Supplemental Insurance (SSI) Is Public Assistance for those Over 65 or the disabled who are not entitled to significant Social Security Benefits.

If you do not qualify for Social Security retirement benefits or you do but your payment is small and not enough to live on, you may be eligible for SSI or Supplemental Security Income. To collect SSI, you must be at least 65 years old or be disabled and have limited resources and income. You must qualify financially and verify your assets and income on a regular basis. You must be a U.S. citizen or legal resident and live in the United States.

Because SSI offers a disability benefit, there is confusion between the two programs, which given their names is understandable: Social Security Disability and Supplemental Security Disability. But they are two entirely different programs with different funding. With Social Security Disability Insurance, workers pay into the Social Security fund via payroll tax and eligible disabled workers are paid from that fund. Whereas, Supplemental Disability is public assistance (welfare) and is funded by general tax revenues.

Supplemental Security Income eligibility is based on your current financial situation and need, not past earnings. You must provide evidence of your income and assets, or lack thereof, on a regular basis to receive benefits. There is a maximum to how much you can earn and a cap on the value of the assets you may have. Any changes to your status must be reported and may affect your payment amount.

If your Social Security retirement benefit is low, you may qualify for SSI as well. The maximum supplemental payment in 2017 is $735 for an eligible individual and $1,103 for a couple if both are eligible.

I often hear people say they are on Social Security when in fact they are receiving Supplemental Security Income. The same happens with Social Security Disability Insurance and Social Supplemental Disability, even though the two programs are completely separate. Retirement benefits are based on an individual's earnings over the course of their lifetime. They have paid into the system. Supplemental Security Income is public assistance. The recipients are generally at or near the poverty level. SSI is in place to provide the basic necessities to those in need.

If you do not qualify for Social Security, chances are you will not qualify for Medicare. Those on SSI may be eligible for Medicaid.

- SSA: The Social Security Administration handles our national insurance system, which includes retirement, survivor and disability insurance for workers.

- OASI: Old Age and Survivor Insurance pays benefits to retired workers and their survivors.

- DI: Disability Insurance pays benefits to qualified workers with disabilities.

- SSI: Supplemental Security Income provides public assistance (welfare) to the disabled and retirees at or below poverty level. It is a separate agency but is administered by Social Security Administration.

Chapter 3

Who Pays?

Social Security is completely funded by payroll tax, interest earned on investments, and tax collected on Social Security benefits paid to recipients. (Yes, Social Security benefits can be taxed.) None of its funding comes from the United States Federal General Fund. Financially, Social Security is a completely stand-alone program. It is separate from all other government programs, and so is its funding.

Social Security is not part of the national budget and does not contribute to the national debt. It is a completely autonomous program. If Social Security benefits were cut, none of that money would go to offset the national deficit. It would go back into the Social Security Fund, which currently has a $2.8 trillion surplus. By law, this money can only be used for Social Security, and by law, this money must be invested. Currently the Social Security Administration receives about $100 billion per year in interest that is added to the Social Security Fund.

It's important to note that even though you can begin collecting Social Security at 62, Medicare doesn't start until age 65.

If you begin collecting early and no longer have health insurance through your employer, you will need to have an alternate source of medical coverage.

Chapter 4

Who Gets Paid?
Are You Eligible?

The focus of this book is retirement and therefore doesn't cover procedures and benefits for the disabled. Please refer to the disability section of Social Security, www.ssa.gov for more information.

To qualify for retirement benefits you must be at least 62 years old, be a U.S. citizen or legal resident, and have earned 40 credits according to the Social Security system.

In addition to the retiree, there may be family members who are eligible for benefits, including a spouse and unmarried minor children under 18. These are known as auxiliary benefits.

Benefits can be extended to children until age 19, if they are full-time students and have not yet graduated high school. They cannot be enrolled in a college or university.

Minor children may include an adopted child, a stepchild, or dependent grandchildren.

The payment amount a child receives will be calculated at 50% of the benefit of the primary earner at Full Retirement Age.

The benefit the child receives does not decrease the benefit of the retiree.

Spouses may be eligible for benefits at any age if they are caring for a dependent or disabled child. Otherwise, they must be at least 62. They also may be entitled to a payment that equals 50% of the retirees benefit. Spousal payments are subject to early collection reductions and work restrictions.

There is a family maximum of 150% to 180% of what the retiree's payment is. This includes the primary wage earner's payment amount. There is a limit to how much the family can receive as a whole.

Who may be eligible for Social Security when you begin receiving your retirement benefits?

- Your spouse if he or she is 62 or older.

- Your spouse at any age if he or she is caring for a dependent child 16 years or under or a disabled child.

- Your unmarried, dependent, minor children under the age of 18.

Family maximum regulations are very complex, and there are different rules for the family members of retirees, the disabled, and survivors.

Here is a simplified example of what you might expect:

If you, as a retiree, receive a monthly payment of $2,000, your dependent child would be entitled to a 50% payment of $1,000. Your eligible spouse also may be entitled to 50% of your benefit amount. But the family maximum – at 180% – would be $3,600. After deducting the $2,000 paid to the primary wage earner, $1,600 remains. That would be split between the minor child and the spouse. Each would receive $800.00.

*To qualify for retirement benefits you must be at least **62** years old, be a U.S. citizen or legal resident, and have earned **40** credits according to the Social Security system.*

Chapter 5

Full Retirement Age: What's that?

Your Full Retirement Age (FRA) is the key to determining when you are eligible for benefits and how much your payments will be. It is the age that the Social Security Administration deems you eligible for your "full benefit."

The FRA used to be 65 for everybody. Now it depends on the year you were born. If you were born between 1943 and 1954, your FRA is 66. For those born between 1955 and 1959 the age will gradually increase. If you were born in 1960 or after, your FRA is 67.

Age To Receive Full Social Security Benefits
(Called "Full Retirement Age" or "normal retirement age.")

Year of Birth *	Full Retirement Age
1943–1954	66
1955	66 and 2 months
1956	66 and 4 months
1957	66 and 6 months
1958	66 and 8 months
1959	66 and 10 months
1960 and later	67

Once you know your FRA, you can consider the best time to apply for benefits. If you apply before your FRA, you will get a smaller monthly payment permanently. If you apply after your FRA, you will get a larger payment for the rest of your life.

Your Full Retirement Age is the center point when determining how much your payment amount will be. Anything before that is considered collecting benefits early. Anything after that is considered collecting benefits late. The changes to your payments last for the rest of your life and therefore the timing of when you apply is crucial to your financial well-being as you age. You'll need to consider it very carefully.

Chapter 6

Should You Apply at 62?

There are several factors you need to consider when deciding the best time to begin collecting Social Security. You can begin collecting anytime between the ages of 62 and 70. There is no increase to your benefit after you reach age 70, so there is no reason to wait any longer.

- The earliest you can apply is 62.

- You can apply after age 70, but there will be no further increase to your payment.

- When you apply *before* your FRA, your payment will be *reduced*. If you apply *after* your FRA, your payment will be *increased*.

- If you were born in 1960 or after, your FRA is 67.

If you begin collecting benefits before your Full Retire-ment Age, your payments will be reduced as follows:

Age	FRA 66	FRA 67
62	25%	30%
63	20%	25%
64	13.3%	20%
65	6.7%	13.3%
66	0%	6.7%

To clarify, Full Retirement Age is when you are eligible for what is considered your "normal" payment. You are receiving 100% of the benefit that Social Security has determined you are entitled to. Anytime you apply before your FRA, you get less. Anytime after FRA, up until age 70, you get more.

For example, if your monthly payment amount at FRA would be $2,000, at 62 your payment would go down to $1,500 for the remainder of your life. If you wait until age 70, your payment would go up to $2,640 for life. That's an increase of $1,140 a month by waiting those eight years.

These adjustments to your payments are permanent. However, you are permitted to change your mind once if you have applied before your FRA. Once you have begun collecting payments, you can withdraw your application within 12 months. But you will have to return the total amount of the payments you received.

Therefore, deciding when to apply will be the biggest decision you make regarding Social Security. Your choice affects your monthly payment amount and that of your family's for the rest of your lives.

Delayed Retirement Credits

If you wait to collect until after your FRA, you accumulate what are known as Delayed Retirement Credits. These credits will increase your monthly payment by 8% per year until age 70, for a total of 32%.

If you are applying for Social Security for the first time, and it is at least six months after you have reached your FRA, you may be eligible to receive up to six months retroactive payments. Please note that if you take the retroactive payments and you have accumulated Delayed Retirement Credits, you will lose the amount your payment increased over those six months permanently.

Once you have reached your Full Retirement Age, you are able to suspend and reactivate your payments at any time.

Wait Until 70?

Financial planners and advisors highly recommend that you wait until age 70 to collect so that you will get the highest payment amount when you are older. It's also worth considering that if you did begin collecting at age 62, over the eight years between 62 and 70 you would have received more than $134,000 in payments. (Based on $2,000 monthly payment amount at FRA.)

The breakeven point between collecting at 62 and 70 is about 80 years old. *You must reach at least 80 to make waiting until 70 pay off.* According to the CDC, the average lifespan for American women is 81, and 76 for men. If you make it to 65, the average goes up to 85 for women and 83 for men. You'll have to weigh the odds.

How do you decide when to apply for Social Security? One of the biggest factors is longevity, but it's impossible to know how long you are going to live. It's a critical question with no solid answer.

Chapter 7

How Long Do You Need to Provide for Yourself?

How Long Will You Live?

Longevity is the wild card when figuring out the best time to apply for benefits and deserves serious consideration.

More people are living into their 90s. What is the likelihood of that for you? You need to estimate how long your money needs to last.

Aside from age and gender, consider how long your family members live. Do your relatives generally live into their 80s or 90s? Is there family history of major illnesses? Your genetics may reflect on your lifespan, too.

What is your personal history? Have you suffered major illnesses, serious accidents, or had surgeries? Do you take care of yourself? Did you drink or smoke? Are you overweight? Active?

Are you married? Those that are in a committed relationship tend to live longer than those that are not. Married individuals take better care of themselves and suffer less from loneliness and depression.

Education and socioeconomic status also affect your lifespan. Exposure to information on healthy lifestyle choices and access to proper medical care and good food can lengthen one's life expectancy.

All of these factors help determine your lifespan and therefore, help you decide when to begin collecting Social Security. There's no way to know for sure how long you're going to be here on this earth. You can only look at the whole picture and make your best guess.

Steps:

- Consider your genetics and family history.

- Consider your personal medical history.

- Examine your personal lifestyle.

- Are you married?

- What is your level of education?

- What is your socioeconomic status?

- Consider your outlook on life. Do you have a positive attitude?

Longevity is a critical factor in determining the best time for you to apply for Social Security benefits. Keep this in mind when contemplating this big step.

If you decide to work, Social Security includes only your wages or net earnings, including bonuses, commissions, and vacation pay as earnings. Retirement plan income, investment earnings, and interest are not included.

Chapter 8

How is your Benefit Amount Determined?

To calculate your benefit, the Social Security Administration will take your 35 highest earning years as reported to the Internal Revenue Service, put them into a formula, and determine your Primary Insurance Amount (PIA), which is your payment amount. The formula that follows comes directly from the Social Security Administration website.

PIA formula:

For an individual who first becomes eligible for old-age insurance benefits or disability insurance benefits in 2016, his/her PIA will be the sum of:

> a. 90 percent of the first $856 of his/her average indexed monthly earnings, plus

b. 32 percent of his/her average indexed monthly earnings over $856 and through $5,157, plus

c. 15 percent of his/her average indexed monthly earnings over $5,157.

This ensures that lower wage earners receive a higher percentage of return on their contributions and is designed so that the majority of workers will have sufficient funds to stay above the poverty level. Women may benefit from this formula because they generally earn less than men and also take more time off from the workforce for family purposes, thereby having a lower overall contribution.

At any age after applying, should you earn more in a year than the previous 35 highest earning years, your benefit amount will increase to reflect the change.

What Will Your Monthly Payment Be?

Social Security has excellent tools for you to determine your approximate benefit amount at ssa.gov. It also sends out periodic notices with your lifetime earning history and estimated benefit at that point in time. The earnings statement will assume that you will continue working at your current income and work until your Full Retirement Age, but also will give estimates for your benefit amount should you decide to start collecting at 62 and 70.

With the estimator, you can enter different salaries and ages and see what your benefit will be at any point in time. The most significant ages are 62, 66, and 70, but you can apply at any time between the ages of 62 and 70. Knowing your benefit amount at different ages can help you determine the best time for you to begin collecting Social Security.

You can determine your approximate monthly payment amount at this point in your life and estimate future payments by:

- going online to ssa.gov.

- opening your My Social Security account.

- requesting your earning statement.

- using the benefit estimator.

If you don't have a computer or would prefer not to open an account, you can order your earnings statement over the phone via an automated system, and it will be mailed to you. Call 1-800-772-1213.

On your statement, you will see your entire lifetime working history according to the IRS. You can verify that the amounts are correct, if you have documentation for those years. You can also see the total amount you have contributed over your working lifetime and how much your employers have paid. Think your employers have paid their share? Think again.

If you have reached your Full Retirement Age, you can work and earn as much as you choose without penalty and still collect your full monthly Social Security benefit. This is true for any age after FRA.

Chapter 9

Can You Work and Collect Social Security?

Yes, you can! You can work and collect Social Security at the same time.

If you have reached your Full Retirement Age, you can work and earn as much as you choose without penalty and still collect your full monthly Social Security benefit. This is true for any age after FRA.

If you are *under* your FRA, however, there is a penalty for anything you earn over $16,920 per year. This is called the earnings test.

If you work and are under your FRA, there is a $1 penalty for every $2 you earn over $16,920.

For instance, if you are 62, collecting Social Security payments and earn $30,920 in a year, you will have earned $14,000 over the limit. Your penalty would be $7,000 and you would also have an additional $7,000 in your pocket.

Whether or not you will work may be the most influential factor when deciding when to begin collecting Social Security.

If you are going to work, you must consider how much you will earn and decide whether it is best for you to wait until your earnings decrease to begin collecting.

Remember too, that you have 12 months to withdraw your application. If your circumstances change, and you are earning more than anticipated, you can withdraw your application, return any Social Security benefits you have been paid, and avoid the penalty. You can then reapply at a later date that is more financially suitable for you.

What Constitutes Income?

For the earnings test, Social Security includes only your wages or net earnings, including bonuses, commissions, and vacation pay. Retirement plan income, investment earnings, and interest are not included.

It's important to note that the penalty is not assessed at the time you earn it, but after you file your tax return. Unless you pay it upfront, it is deducted from your monthly Social Security payment. Your payment will be withheld until the penalty is satisfied. If you owe $7,000 and your monthly payment is $1,400, you may not receive a Social Security check for *five* months at some time in the future. The penalty may not be taken out immediately, but rest assured it will be taken out eventually. Don't get caught by surprise. Calculate for this in your budget.

Also, if your payment is withheld because of work, anyone else receiving benefits on your work record—your spouse and minor child—will have their payments suspended as well. But the work of others collecting on your account does not affect anyone else's benefit, including your own.

If you plan on working full time and making more than $16,920, you may want to wait until your Full Retirement Age to apply for Social Security benefits. Most or all of your payment could go to pay the penalties.

In the year of your Full Retirement Age, the penalty and maximum you can earn changes. The amount you can earn before you are penalized is $44,880 in 2017. If you made more than that, the penalty is decreased to $1 for every $3 you earned.

After your FRA, there is no limit and there is no penalty.

The earning limits are calculated on a full calendar year, January to December, not from when you start collecting.

If you have been penalized for earning over the allowed limit, once you reach FRA, your benefit will be recalculated with those months included and will result in an increase in your monthly payment. It may take 10 to 15 years to make up the amount lost due to the penalties.

If you have earned more in any recent year than in one of your previous 35 years, Social Security will re-calculate your benefit automatically. It will replace a past lower earning year with a current higher earning year, thereby increasing your monthly payment.

Once you reach your FRA, there is no limit to the amount you can earn. There is no longer a penalty at any time in the future.

Chapter 10

Is Social Security Taxed?

Federal Tax on Social Security

Social Security benefits are considered income by the Internal Revenue Service and are subject to federal tax. The tax rate depends on your total income and tax bracket. For individuals, if your combined income is greater than $25,000, you must pay tax on a certain amount of your benefit. If you file a joint return and your combined income exceeds $32,000, you will be required to pay tax.

If your payment is at or near the minimum, it is unlikely you will need to pay any tax on it. You will never need to pay tax on more than 85% of your benefit.

For federal tax purposes, your "combined income" includes your adjusted gross income, tax-exempt interest income, and half of your Social Security benefits.

Any tax collected by the IRS on Social Security goes back into the Social Security fund. It does not go into the general fund.

States that Tax Social Security

In addition to federal tax, there are 13 states that tax Social Security. They are Colorado, Connecticut, Kansas, Minnesota, Missouri, Montana, Nebraska, New Mexico, North Dakota, Rhode Island, Utah, Vermont, and West Virginia.

The other 37 states do not. This makes them attractive to retirees on a budget. Each state has its own tax rate for retirement income, and many offer exemptions for those who don't make over a certain amount.

For example, if you retire in Missouri, individuals are allowed to make $85,000 from all income sources, including Social Security, before you have to pay state taxes. The amount increases to $100,000 for married couples. Check your state to see what rules apply.

Payroll Tax

People often ask, "When will they stop taking Social Security tax out of my paycheck?" Believe it or not, as long as you are earning money, you are required to pay a percentage of your earnings to Social Security via the payroll tax. This applies even if you are collecting Social Security and are past your FRA. Payroll tax never ends.

Taxes on Social Security benefits are currently a reality and something that you need to take into consideration when deciding when to apply for Social Security benefits. If you are in a high tax bracket for a particular year, you may want to consider waiting until your taxable income is lower.

For federal tax purposes, your "combined income" includes your adjusted gross income, tax-exempt interest income, and half of your Social Security benefits.

Chapter 11

What if You Are Married?

Married Couples

For most married couples today, both individuals have earned enough on their own record to be eligible for Social Security payments, but they may also be eligible for benefits on their spouse's record. If you are eligible for both, here's how Social Security calculates your payment amount. Payment on your own record is based on 100% of your calculated benefit amount if you have reached your Full Retirement Age. A spousal benefit is 50% of the higher wage-earner's benefit. Basically, you will receive the equivalent of the higher of the two amounts.

A spousal benefit is 50% of the higher wage-earner's benefit amount. For example, if Joe's monthly payment is $2,000 at Full Retirement Age, his wife Ann's payment will be 50% of that – $1,000 – at her Full Retirement Age. They would receive a total of $3,000 per month.

If either Joe or Ann collects before FRA, their payments will be reduced as much as 30%. If Joe collects $2,000, Ann is eligible to receive $1,000 at her FRA. If she begins collecting spousal benefits at 62, she will receive about $700.

If Ann is entitled to $1,500 per month on her own account, she will not be eligible for a spousal benefit because hers is higher than the $1,000 she would otherwise receive.

If you are married and were born after January 1, 1954, when you file Social Security will consider you are applying for both your own benefit and spousal benefits. You will receive the higher of the two.

If you receive a spouse's benefit, it does not decrease the payment amount of the higher earner. It is in addition to it. In the example cited, Joe, the higher wage earner, receives $2,000 per month and Ann is entitled to $1,000 per month. Together they receive $3,000.

A single person who has earned the same amount as Joe receives only his or her benefit of $2,000.

In order to provide the highest payment amount available to a surviving spouse, many couples seek to maximize the primary wage-earner's payment by waiting as long as possible to collect. When one spouse dies, the survivor gets only one payment – on their own record or the spouse's record, whichever is higher.

When a spouse passes away, the survivor receives only one Social Security check from that point forward. If as a couple you were each receiving a check, you would now receive only one check, the higher of the two payments. If you are receiving $1,000 and your spouse is receiving $2,000, at death the remaining spouse will receive one check for $2,000 each month.

Women generally live longer than men, and losing a payment can be a great financial burden at a difficult time. Not only does one lose a partner, but also a significant amount of income. This is when many elderly women struggle and fall below the poverty level.

Deciding when to apply and collect Social Security benefits can be a complicated decision. There are many factors and the stakes are high. As a married couple, you may want to make this decision together so that you receive the highest amount available at the time you need it most.

The Basic Rules of Spousal Benefits

Spousal Benefits provide additional income for couples as they age. When a primary wage earner begins collecting Social Security, his or her spouse may become eligible to receive payments as well. Even if spouses have earned no income or very little, they still may be eligible for retirement benefits. Once you qualify for Social Security benefits, you and your spouse will qualify for Medicare at age 65.

To collect spousal benefits:

- You must be at least 62 years of age.

- Your spouse must have filed for and be receiving retirement benefits.

- Benefits on your own record must be less than what you would receive as a spouse.

- You must have been married for at least one year.

- Only one individual of a married couple can collect spousal benefits.

Your age and how much you have earned in your lifetime will determine your eligibility for spousal benefits and the amount of your payment.

If you *have* earned enough to be eligible for benefits on your own record and your monthly payment will be *higher* than what you would collect from spousal benefit, you will receive payment based on your own record and will not receive spousal benefits.

If you *have* earned enough on your own record to be eligible for benefits but your monthly payment will be *lower* than what you would collect in a spousal benefit, you will receive your benefit plus the difference between the two to make your total payment the equivalent of the spousal benefit.

If you *have not* earned enough on your own record to be eligible for benefits, you will receive 50% of your spouse's payment amount at Full Retirement Age.

If you begin collecting benefits in any of these scenarios before your FRA, the amount of your payment will be reduced.

If you are married and were born after January 1, 1954, when you file Social Security will consider you are applying for both your own benefit and spousal benefits. You will receive the higher of the two.

Whether you are single or married, if you take benefits early, your payment amount will be reduced.

Chapter 12

What if I'm Divorced?

Can I Collect Spousal Benefits If I Am Divorced?

Many divorced individuals are surprised to learn they can collect Social Security on their ex-spouse's record. This is important since men often earn more than women. Divorced women may be able to get a higher payment by applying for spousal or survivor benefits on their ex-husband's record.

To be eligible for spousal benefits when you are divorced:

- You must have been married for at least 10 years.

- You must be unmarried.

- You must be divorced two years or more.

- You must be at least 62.

- Your former spouse must be at least 62.

Unlike married couples, both divorced individuals can collect benefits on each other's work record.

The benefit you are entitled to receive based on your own work must be less than the benefit you would receive based on your ex-spouse's work.

Important Details for the Divorced:

The maximum amount of your benefit is 50% of what your former spouse would receive at Full Retirement Age. Unlike a married couple, your ex-spouse must qualify for benefits, but does not need to have filed for you to collect.

- The maximum amount of your spousal benefit is 50% of what your former spouse would receive at Full Retirement Age. Unlike a married couple, your ex-spouse must qualify for benefits, but does not need to have filed for you to collect.

- Your award does not affect the amount your former spouse receives. Nor does it affect the benefits of his or her current spouse or eligible child. It is not included in the family maximum.

- If your ex-spouse's payment increases because he or she files after Full Retirement Age, yours does not. Your payment amount is permanent.

- If you begin collecting before your Full Retirement Age, your payment amount will be reduced.

- If you have applied before your Full Retirement Age and continue to work, you will be subject to the earnings test and everything you earn above $16,920 will be penalized.

If at all possible have your marriage certificate, your divorce decree, or other documents proving your marriage and divorce available for Social Security. Having your ex-spouse's Social Security number and date of birth is also helpful.

You may have been married and divorced 30 or 40 years ago and Social Security may not have a record of it, but you still may be eligible for benefits. There is no time limit for spousal and survivor benefits for divorced individuals. You can apply any number of years later. But you must be able to prove that you were married for 10 years or more and divorced for at least two years. This is especially important when considering survivor benefits. You may have earned enough on your own record to keep you from receiving spousal benefits. But if your ex earned more than you, when he or she dies you are entitled to 100% of their benefit. Switching from your own benefit to survivor benefits on your ex-spouse's record could give your Social Security check a nice boost.

Because of privacy laws, Social Security cannot give out information regarding your spouse's record or whether or not they have applied for benefits. They can only reveal if you are eligible for benefits and what that payment would be. There's a very limited amount of information they can tell you.

Chapter 13

Are Same Sex-Couples Eligible for Social Security Benefits?

Same-Sex Couples

Since the Supreme Court ruling of June 26, 2015, same-sex marriages are legal everywhere in the U.S. This ruling ensures that same-sex couples are entitled to the same benefits and are under the same regulations as any other couple. Check with Social Security promptly. Don't miss out on any benefits.

Individuals in a same-sex marriage or legal union are eligible for the same benefits as heterosexual couples. If you are married, joined by a civil union, or domestic partnership, you may be entitled to Social Security benefits on your partner's record. If you are divorced or a survivor of a same-sex couple, you may be entitled to benefits as well. It is recommende that you apply for benefits right away to see what you may be entitled to and to safeguard against loss of any benefits.

When a spouse passes away, the survivor receives only one Social Security check from that point forward.

Chapter **14**

What If My Spouse Has Died?

Survivor Benefits: What if Your Spouse is Deceased?

Social Security provides Survivor Benefits to the family of a deceased worker who has contributed to the system and is eligible for benefits. Spousal Survivor Benefits are paid at 100% of the worker's entitled amount. The payment amount is determined by the contributions of the worker and the age at which he or she passed away.

The surviving spouse may apply for benefits at age 60, but will receive a reduced amount for collecting early. When applying at Full Retirement Age, the surviving spouse will receive 100% of the benefit.

If the surviving spouse remarries before the age of 60, he or she is no longer entitled to the Survivor

Benefit from the previous marriage. Surviving spouses who remarry after age 60 are able to receive the benefit indefinitely, even if a new spouse is collecting his or her own benefit. You also are able to claim survivor benefits while allowing your own benefit to continue to increase, and then switch to your higher benefit later on. This is a major difference with spousal benefits.

Although a divorced spouse can apply at age 60, if you do so before your FRA, your monthly payment amount will be reduced accordingly.

Surviving spouses and children are entitled to a one-time benefit of $255. Other survivors are not.

If a worker dies before he earns 40 credits, depending on their age, they may need fewer credits for the family to receive benefits. The younger the deceased, the fewer credits needed.

Social Security can pay survivor benefits to your children and a spouse who is caring for the children even if you don't have the usually required number of credits needed. The younger you are, the fewer credits you need for your family to get benefits.

General Rules for Survivor Benefits:

- For survivor (spouse) benefits in general, you must be at least 60 years old to apply

- If you remarry before age 60, you are no longer eligible for survivor benefits.

- If you remarry after age 60, you are still eligible for survivor benefits.

- A divorced spouse can receive survivor benefits if they were married for at least 10 years and divorced for two.

- If you apply before your Full Retirement Age, your payment will be reduced.

- If you apply early and continue to work, you will be subject to the earnings test and penalized for earnings over $16,920.

- You can receive survivor benefits early and later switch to your own benefit if it is higher.

- When a spouse passes away, the survivor receives only one Social Security check from that point forward.

Children and Survivor Benefits

Your unmarried, minor children may be able to receive benefits on your record should you die. They must be 18 or younger, 19 if they are a full-time student and not yet graduated from high school. They would receive 75% of the amount of your benefit.

A surviving spouse, at any age, can receive a benefit of 75% of your payment amount if caring for your minor child. Keep in mind that there is a family maximum of 150% to 180% of the worker's payment.

Dependent Parents

If you supplied 50% of support for your mother and/or father, they may be eligible to receive survivor benefits on your work record. They need to be 62 or older and be dependent upon you for at least half of their expenses.

Chapter **15**

Windfall Elimination Provision (WEP)

If you are eligible for a public pension – firefighters, police officers, teachers, and others – and *have not* contributed to Social Security while working at *that* job, and worked at another job where you did contribute to Social Security, you may be subject to the Windfall Elimination Provision.

If you have worked at another job and paid into Social Security and earned at least 40 credits, you are eligible for benefits, but your expected monthly Social Security payment may be reduced significantly. Here's why:

Social Security calculates your benefits by taking your 35 highest earning years. Any years you didn't pay Social Security tax are calculated as zero. If you are a teacher or firefighter, the total amount you contributed over your working lifetime will be low and it will appear that you are a low-income worker when you are not.

As part of the Social Security formula used to calculate your monthly benefit, lower-income individuals receive a higher percentage of their contributions back. This means that the government worker's monthly payment would be calculated at a higher rate than it should because these workers have been contributing to a pension fund and are not actually low income.

The Windfall Elimination Provision prevents government workers from collecting their full pension AND a full Social Security benefit at the same time. The Social Security benefit is recalculated using the proper income level, which lowers the payment.

The real problem here is not the policy, it's that many government workers are not aware of it and don't take it into account when calculating their retirement income. They may receive a statement from Social Security that estimates the higher amount, because Social Security calculates your estimate from the amount of payroll tax you pay. If you are not paying the tax at your current job, Social Security doesn't know you have another source of income.

Each year, there is a maximum amount that your payment will be reduced because of the Windfall Elimination Provision. The amount of your reduction is determined by the number of years you worked and paid into Social Security. For 2016, if you paid Social Security tax for 20 years, the maximum reduction is

$428 per month. The amount is lowered the longer you work.

The decrease is calculated based on your payment amount in the year of your eligibility (age 62 is the earliest) before adjustment because of early or late filing as well as cost of living. The Windfall Elimination will never be more than one half of your pension.

There are many government positions where employees *do* pay into Social Security and the Windfall Elimination Provision *does not* apply. If this is the case, you will get your full Social Security benefit.

Be aware that if you worked internationally and paid into a foreign nation's pension plan, your U.S. Social Security benefits may be subject to this provision as well.

If you are eligible for a public pension and have not contributed to Social Security while working at that job, and worked at another job where you did contribute to Social Security, you may be subject to the Windfall Elimination Provision and your payment may be reduced.

Chapter **16**

Government Pension Offset (GPO)

The Government Pension Offset is similar to the Windfall Elimination Provision in that your Social Security benefit may be reduced. Whereas the WEP affects payments on your own record, the GPO affects a survivor's benefit.

If you worked in a government job and paid into a pension and did not pay into Social Security, when your spouse dies, you do not receive both your pension and your spouse's full Social Security benefit. Social Security will deduct about two-thirds of your pension amount from your survivor benefit.

The logic behind this regulation is that if a married couple both worked in the private sector and both contributed to Social Security, when one passes away the survivor is entitled to only one benefit. Survivors do not get both. They will receive either benefits calculated on their own record or benefits calculated on their spouse's record. They get the higher of the two.

The Government Pension Offset is modeled on that Social Security regulation. It is to ensure there is some parity between the two systems and to make sure no one is receiving two full benefits at one time.

Those subject to the GPO actually make out better than those who are not. The GPO allows the beneficiary to keep a portion of the Social Security survivor benefit (one third of your pension amount), while those not subject to it lose one benefit entirely.

A problem with both the Windfall Elimination Provision and the Government Pension Offset is that many workers are not aware of these rules, and they overestimate their retirement income. This can have grave consequences on the financial status and retirement lifestyle of an individual or a surviving spouse.

If you worked in a government job and paid into a pension and did not pay into Social Security, when your spouse dies, you do not receive both your pension and your spouse's full Social Security benefit.

Chapter 17

How Can You Apply?

Is Applying Easy?

For most people applying for Social Security benefits, it's pretty easy. You can apply online, over the phone, or in person at your local Social Security office.

Online

To apply online, go to ssa.gov and open a "My Social Security" account. If you are over 62, you will have access to the application. The application takes about 15 to 30 minutes to complete. Before you begin filling out the application, it is recommended you know the following:

- Your Full Retirement Age.

- The consequences of applying early.

- If you will work and how much you can earn without penalty.

- Your approximate life expectancy, as much as you are able to estimate.

Have these documents available:

- Passport or birth certificate if a US citizen.

- Green card if you are a resident alien.

- Marriage certificate for spousal benefit.

- Divorce decree if appropriate.

- Bank information to set up direct deposit.

You don't have to fill out the application in one sitting. You can save it and come back to it later.

By Phone

Call 1-800-772-1213. You can then make a specific appointment to complete your application with an agent over the phone.

In Person

You can find the nearest Social Security location online or from the main number, 1-800-772-1213. You can then make an appointment to have an agent assist you in filling out your application. If applying in person, you must bring the originals of the above mentioned documents. Copies are not accepted.

When asking for information from a Social Security Agent, whether online, by telephone, or in person, it's always best to verify the information. Budgets have been cut, and agents are under a lot of stress. Many people report getting the wrong information. This can cause you to make decisions that are not in your best interest and lose a great deal of money over time.

Learn the regulations about your particular situation before you apply. If you are given information that doesn't sound right to you, ask to speak to a supervisor.

You can apply online, over the phone, or in person at your local Social Security office.

Chapter 18

Can You Collect Social Security While Living Abroad?

Yes, you can! There are many countries where you can reside and collect your Social Security without much trouble, but there are a few exceptions. Also the U.S. has treaties with many nations that may affect how your Social Security benefits are received and possibly taxed.

Countries Where You May Not Be Able to Receive Checks

You can collect Social Security payments almost anywhere in the world. The most notable exceptions are North Korea and Cuba. With the 2016 appointment of an ambassador to Cuba, this status may soon change. Currently, if you live in either North Korea or Cuba, you cannot receive payments while you are there. If you are a U.S. citizen, you can collect any payments you have missed once you leave those countries.

Social Security does not usually send payments to individuals residing in the following countries: Azerbaijan, Belarus, Georgia, Kazakhstan, Kyrgyzstan, Moldova, Tajikistan, Turkmenistan, Ukraine, and Uzbekistan. Exceptions can be made, but restrictions do apply. You may have to verify your presence by appearing at the U.S. Embassy or Consulate every three months.

Countries Where You Can Receive Checks

The U.S. has treaties with 25 countries in which you will receive your Social Security payments without problems regardless of how long you stay. They are: Austria, Belgium, Canada, Chile, Czech Republic, Finland, France, Germany, Greece, Hungary, Ireland, Israel, Italy, Japan, South Korea, Luxembourg, the Netherlands, Norway, Poland, Portugal, Slovak Republic, Spain, Sweden, Switzerland, and the United Kingdom. These treaties can protect you from having your income taxed in both the U.S. and the foreign nation where you reside.

You can receive payments in most other countries, but you may be subject to specific rules and regulations. Social Security has a "Payments Abroad Screening Tool" that will tell you if you can receive payments in a specific country by answering a few simple questions.

With electronic banking and international direct deposit, receiving your benefits abroad has never been easier. By keeping an American bank account, you can avoid mishaps that may delay access to your funds at a local bank. Depending on the country, it can be challenging to open a local bank account. You often need referrals, documentation from other institutions, and proof of a local address. Sometimes these can be difficult to obtain when you are new to an area.

The U.S. has various treaties with numerous countries regarding international banking. It's always good to verify the circumstances and procedures for receiving Social Security payments in any nation you plan to live.

It is important when living abroad that you keep your contact information up to date with the U.S. Embassy or Consulate so that you can be informed of local dangers, crisis, contacted in an emergency, and possibly evacuated if need be.

Foreign Spouses and Their Benefits

Non-citizen spouses that have lived in the United States as part of a married couple for five years or more may be able to receive spousal or survivor benefits while living abroad without needing to return to the U.S. If the spouse has not lived in the U.S. for five years, they may need to return to the U.S. every six months in order for payments to continue. Payments will stop when the spouse has been out of the country for six consecutive months. Payments may be reinstated if the eligible spouse returns for one full month (not 30 days). If the spouse resides in a country with which the U.S. has a Social Security agreement, then they may be able to receive benefits without having to return to the U.S.

Living Abroad and Taxes

Regardless of where U.S. citizens reside, they are required to file a tax return with the Internal Revenue Service. Social Security benefits are considered income and will be taxed by the U.S. government where applicable. You may also be required to pay tax to the country in which you live.

For individuals, if your combined income is greater than $25,000, you must pay tax on a certain amount of your benefit. If you file a joint return and your combined income exceeds $32,000, you will be required to pay tax. For federal tax purposes, your "combined income" includes your adjusted gross income, tax-exempt interest income, and half of your Social Security benefits. You will never need to pay tax on more than 85% of your benefit.

In addition to U.S. taxes, you may be required to pay tax to the country where you live. The U.S. has treaties with many countries that avoid this double taxation for both our citizens and theirs.

Working In a Foreign Country

The laws regarding working or owning a business in a foreign nation will vary from country to country. You'll need to investigate what they are in the specific country where you live. Should you work or own a business in a foreign country, you must report it to Social Security. Your income will be subject to the same means test as those who live in the United States. If you earn more than $16,920 per year, additional earnings will be taxed $1 for every $2 you earn.

For more information, go to
ssa.gov/international/payments.html

Retiring overseas can be a wonderful experience. A lower cost of living, the culture, language, arts and climate can be especially appealing. It's comforting to know that you can receive the benefits you have paid for almost anywhere in the world you choose to live. Bon voyage!

Non-citizen spouses that have lived in the United States as part of a married couple may be able to receive spousal or survivor benefits while living abroad.

Chapter **19**

Social Security and Women

What women should know about Social Security

Social Security is designed to be gender neutral, but can still be unfair to women. It wasn't intended to be, but things have changed over time. Women no longer stay at home much of their adult lives. They work. At work, they generally earn less than men. Since your Social Security payment is based on your earnings, lower lifetime earnings results in a lower Social Security payment.

Not only do women generally earn less than men over their lifetimes, they are more likely to take extended time off to raise a family. Any years not worked will be calculated as a zero. This can bring your monthly payment down significantly.

Social Security pays on a curve: lower income workers receive a higher percentage of their salary as their payment. This was designed so that those with a lower income would have a large enough payment to stay above the poverty level and to provide all workers with the basic necessities as they age. The curve in the formula may help to bridge the earnings gap for women, but not completely.

An unmarried woman who works will get a lower overall payment than a married man who earns the same amount over the same number of years. If a single woman is entitled to a $2,000 monthly payment and a married man is entitled to $2,000, his wife also is entitled to $1,000 in spousal benefit for a total of $3,000.

Get Married

It is common now for couples to live together and not get married. That piece of paper may not mean much to you, but it means a lot to Social Security. Should your mate become disabled or die, you have no recourse to collect benefits on his or her account. This is especially important if you have children. They may get benefits on their deceased parent's account, but you won't. That additional payment could be essential in making ends meet.

If you plan on staying together, consider getting married. It can make a big difference in your quality of life when you are older due to spousal and survivor benefits. There is an accepted notion that if you live together for seven years you have a common law marriage. This is not true in most places in the United States. Several states do recognize common law marriages, but the requirements vary and are not usually dependent on the length of time you are together. For Social Security purposes, you will need to prove you were legally married according to the laws of your state.

If you do not qualify for Social Security, you will not automatically qualify for Medicare. If your spouse is eligible for Medicare in most cases, you are, too.

If you are divorced, you can collect spousal or survivor benefits if you were married for at least 10 years. If your spouse's earnings were higher than yours, you can increase your Social Security payment after he dies.

Getting married sooner will increase the likelihood that you are married for 10 years or more. It doesn't count if you live together for five years and are married for five years.

If you are contemplating divorce and income on your own record is low, you may want to postpone the final divorce decree until you have reached 10 years. This way you will be entitled to spousal and survivor benefits, which may be much higher than what you would receive on your own record. This could offer you a better standard of living and nicer lifestyle as you get older.

My friend, Sylvia, and her ex-husband Tom were together for 15 years. He earned considerably more than she did, but they were only married for seven years. He remarried and she did not. She's lived on one income and hasn't been able to save. Because of her low earnings, she will not get a large monthly Social Security payment. Because they were married for less than 10 years, she is not entitled to any benefits on his record.

Don't be lulled into thinking you don't have to worry because you will have your spouse's Social Security to rely on. With a 50% divorce rate and spousal support being only 50% of your spouse's payment amount, you could end up getting the short end of the stick. It's better to be prepared. The worst that could happen is you have more money for your retirement.

After all, according to Social Security "17.3% of non-married elderly women (widowed, divorced, never married) are living in poverty today." Think ahead. Don't be one of them!

- Be prepared, know the law.

- Get married.

- Stay married for 10 years.

- Pay your payroll taxes. Don't work off the books or if you work for yourself, make sure you declare your income.

- Earn enough on your own record to qualify for both Social Security and Medicare.

Other Recommendations for Women

- When you are young, open a Roth IRA so that you have your own account accumulating funds throughout your lifetime.

- Get a traditional IRA in your name based on your spouse's earnings record throughout the time you take off to raise a family. This can help make up for your loss in Social Security benefits for that time out of the workplace.

According to Social Security 17.3% of non-married elderly women (widowed, divorced, never married) are living in poverty today.

Chapter **20**

What is the Best Time to Begin Collecting Social Security?

Trying to determine the best time to collect Social Security is a difficult undertaking that will depend on your personal circumstances and desires. You can collect any time between 62 and 70 but you'll want to consider several factors. Can you pay your bills without Social Security, or do you need the money now? Are you going to work? And are you going to earn more than $16,920 a year? This is a critical question when deciding when to collect Social Security benefits considering the penalty involved.

How long will you live? Consider your family and personal medical history. How long do you have to provide for yourself?

What do you want? Do you want to stop working and spend time with the grandchildren, go fishing, or just enjoy the things you love to do? Many people feel these years may be the best they have left and they want to spend them enjoying themselves. I might take benefits early and not work for four years and travel. When I reach my Full Retirement Age, I can work without losing any income and feel OK about not having missed out on anything.

Consider:

- How long will you continue to work?

- Do you have a source of health insurance until you are 65 and Medicare starts?

- Can you pay your bills? Do you need the income from Social Security now?

- What is your personal and family medical history? How long do you have to provide for yourself?

- Do you want to enjoy these years as they may be the best you have left?

- What about family? If your spouse and dependent children can only collect when you are collecting, you may have to consider what is best for all of you.

Deciding when to apply and collect Social Security benefits can be a complicated decision. There are many factors and a lot at stake. Your financial situation, employment choices, assets, tax brackets, health, and expected Social Security payment amounts must all be considered in order to make the best choice.

There's no blanket right or wrong time to begin collecting Social Security. There is only the right time for *you*.

PART 2

Changes Due to
The Bipartisan Budget
Act of 2015

Chapter 21

The File and Suspend

Previously, one wage earner in a couple would file for benefits at Full Retirement Age. Filing made their spouse eligible to begin collecting spousal benefits. The primary wage earner could then suspend receiving payments, which allowed his or her future benefit amount to continue to increase 8% per year until age 70. At the same time, the spouse – at Full Retirement Age – would collect spousal benefits, which could amount to as much as $63,000 over those four years.

Under the new rule, you can still file and suspend and get the increase, but you must be collecting payments in order for your spouse to receive benefits on your account. If you suspend your payment, you suspend for both of you. This does not apply to divorced spouses.

In the past, an eligible spouse could receive 50% of the primary earner's benefit amount while their payment was suspended, and the future benefit continued to increase 8% each year. Now, a couple gets one or the other. They can wait and get the 8% per year increase on the primary earner's benefit and not collect the spousal benefit (neither would be receiving any payment from Social Security), or they can begin collecting both the primary wage earner's benefit and the associated spousal benefit and forfeit the 8% increase.

If you currently have filed and suspended or are collecting benefits on another person's record, you are grandfathered in and will not lose your benefits.

If you were born on or before April 30, 1950, you were able to file and suspend before May 1, 2016 and release benefits for others eligible to receive payment on your work record.

If you were born after April 30, 1950, you are able to file and suspend, but you will suspend benefits for others able to receive payments on your work record, including your spouse.

Chapter 22

The Restricted Application

In relation to the file and suspend strategy, the person applying for spousal benefits would file a restricted application at Full Retirement Age. This means the application was restricted to spousal benefits and did not include benefits on his or her own record.

While collecting spousal benefits, the payment amount on the filer's own record would increase 8% per year. At age 70, this individual would switch from receiving spousal benefits to receiving benefits on his or her own record, which would now have increased by 32%. This higher payment would be paid for the remainder of their life.

Filing a restricted application is not available to those born January 2, 1954 or after. Those who are eligible can only file a restricted application if you have reached your Full Retirement Age.

If you currently have filed and suspended or are collecting benefits on another person's record, you are grandfathered in and will not lose your benefits.

If you were born on or before January 1, 1954, you are able to file a restricted application at your Full Retirement Age and collect spousal benefits while your own benefits are increasing 8% per year.

You can later switch to benefits on your own record, which may now be higher than what you receive as a spousal benefit.

If you were born on January 2, 1954 or after, you are not eligible to file a restricted application. You will not be able to switch from a spousal benefit to one on your own record with the exception of a survivor benefit.

Chapter 23

The Claim and Switch

Filing a restricted application and claiming one benefit (spousal) and later switching to another (your own) is called the claim and switch. It is this strategy that Congress objected to as unfair when making changes through the Bipartisan Budget Act of 2015, which was signed into law on November 2, 2015.

- If you were born on or before January 1, 1954, you may file for spousal benefits at your Full Retirement Age, and later switch to benefits on your own record. Benefits on your own record will have continued to increase at 8% per year, while you have been receiving 50% of the amount of your spouse's benefit.

- If you were born on or before January 1, 1954 (age 62 in 2015), you may still file for spousal benefits at age 66 (four years from now) and then switch to your own benefit at age 70.

- If you were born on or after January 2, 1954, when you apply for benefits you will get the higher of your benefit and the spousal benefit you are eligible for. And it's over. Your benefit will no longer increase 8% per year and you cannot switch from one benefit to the other.

As you can see, the File and Suspend, Restricted Application, and the Claim and Switch all worked together to make collecting two benefits possible. Many are sorry to see it go, but most Social Security experts believe it was an unintended loophole that was unfairly taken advantage of.

Conclusion

We all have our hopes and dreams about retirement. It may be sitting on a beach, playing golf, traveling or spending more time with friends and family.

The fears we have about planning for retirement can be overwhelming. It's important not to let them overshadow the remarkable things we may have in store for us.

Learning the rules and regulations of Social Security and Medicare can lessen those fears. These programs are the backbone of the financial existence of many retirees, and it's important to understand them so that you can get what you are entitled to.

I wrote this book with the hope of making these programs less intimidating and manageable for you. Knowing how they work can give you the confidence you need to feel that you are making the best choices for you and your family.

If you've found this book valuable, please tell your friends and family. There are so many people who make mistakes that hurt them financially. Let's help as many as possible.

I wish you a very happy, satisfying retirement.

Bonus Section

MEDICARE

Chapter 1

Eligibility

Medicare is the national health insurance plan for workers in the United States age 65 or older. You pay into the plan with payroll taxes. A small portion of your earnings, 1.45%, are deducted from each of your paychecks. Your employer matches that amount for a total contribution of 2.9% in your name. There is no cap to Medicare tax. You pay tax on your total earnings no matter how high.

Unlike Social Security, which is totally autonomous and not part of the national budget or deficit, Medicare is subsidized. Part A is paid for entirely by tax revenues. Part B and D are paid for by premiums and Federal subsidies.

To qualify for Medicare, you must have been a legal resident of the United States for five consecutive years and paid Medicare tax for at least 10 years and earned 40 Social Security credits. If you qualify for Social Security retirement benefits, you will qualify for Medicare. Spouses, ex-spouses, and widows of eligible workers may be covered as well.

Eligibility Requirements for Medicare

- You must be 65 or older.

- You must be a U.S. citizen or legal resident.

- You must have lived in the U.S. for at least five consecutive years.

- You must have worked for at least 10 years and earned 40 Social Security credits.

You have paid for Medicare with a portion of your paycheck your entire working life. Medicare is not public assistance. It is not welfare or Medicaid. You have contributed your money into a program to ensure you have health care as you age.

It's important to know that although you can begin collecting Social Security at age 62, Medicare coverage begins at 65. If you choose to receive Social Security before your 65th birthday, you will need another source of medical insurance until then. This can be a major factor in deciding when to start collecting Social Security.

If you are eligible for Social Security, you should receive your Medicare card in the mail three months before your 65th birthday. This will provide coverage of Part A and Part B. Part B is optional. You will also receive information on how to reject Part B if you choose to do so. Contact Medicare if you do not receive your card.

Medicare is not free. There are premiums, de-duct-ibles, and co-pays like other insurance plans. Medi-care covers an average of 48% of your total health care expenses; therefore, 52% will be your respon-sibility. You can purchase supplemental (Medigap) policies that cover more of your care. There will be an additional premium.

It is important to know what costs you are expect-ed to pay and how you will pay for them before you agree to services. One third of bankruptcies by se-nior citizens are due to medical expenses.

You do not need to be collecting Social Security to be covered by Medicare.

Chapter 2

Part A

Medicare is divided into four parts: Part A, B, C, and D. Each part covers different services.

Part A

- Part A covers hospital care if you are formally admitted and require a stay longer than two nights.

- Your treatment must be medically necessary and must require in-patient care.

- There is no premium for Part A if you have been a legal resident of the U.S. for at least five years and have earned 40 Social Security credits.

- Part A has a deductible of $1,316 per benefit period.

- If you do not qualify, you may obtain coverage by paying a premium of up to $413 per month.

The Part A "benefit period" is not a calendar year. It begins when you are admitted as an inpatient to a hospital, long-term care facility, or skilled nursing facility. It ends when you have not received in-patient care for 60 consecutive days. After the 60 days, a new benefit period begins and you are subject to another $1,316 deductible. You also then begin at day 1 for hospital coverage and have 60 days of care without a co-pay. You may have more than one benefit period per year.

In summary, Part A:

- Covers you for in-patient hospital care.

- Has no premium if you qualify.

- Has a $1,316 deductible per benefit period.

- May have more than one benefit period in a year and you may have to pay more than one deductible in a year.

- Does not cover emergency room care.

Hospital Care

After your deductible is met, there is no co-pay your first 60 days in a hospital. Days 61–90 there is a

$329 per day co-pay. After 90 days in a benefit period, you are entitled to 60 "Lifetime Reserve Days." These have a co-pay of $658 per day. Beyond your "Lifetime Reserve Days," the patient is responsible for all costs.

- First 60 days: no co-pay

- 61–90 days: $329 per day co-pay

- 60 "Lifetime Reserve Days:" $658 per day co-pay

The average overnight hospital cost per day in the United States is more than $2,000. The cost per state varies widely.

Long-Term Care

Not to be confused with long-term care insurance, long-term care is subject to the same limitations and charges as acute care. The number of days listed in the Hospital Care section is a total of your combined stay in a hospital or other covered facility.

If you have a serious condition that requires medically necessary care over a long period of time and you are expected to recover, you may be eligible for long-term care coverage.

Your deductible is per benefit period. You do not pay an additional deductible if you change facilities.

Skilled Nursing Services

Medicare Part A covers services provided in a "skilled nursing facility." This would include physical and occupational therapy and speech pathology services. Medication, medical supplies, and equipment needed while you are an in-patient are also covered.

In order to have your stay in a skilled nursing facility paid for by Medicare, you must have a qualifying hospital stay of three consecutive days or more as an inpatient and a doctor's approval that you need more care. Your deductible for the benefit period will already have been applied during your hospital stay.

The first 20 days per benefit period in a skilled nursing facility are paid at 100% for covered services. For days 21–100, there is a charge of $164.50 co-pay per day. Days 101 and after are the full responsibility of the patient.

Homecare

Medicare Part A and Part B together cover homecare if your doctor has certified that you are homebound and that your treatment is medically necessary. Physical therapy, speech pathology, or occupational therapy may be covered. Your condition must be expected to improve within a certain period of time. The services provided must require a skilled therapist and the associated agency must be Medicare-certified. Medicare does not cover 24-hour care.

Medicare does not cover help with daily activities of living such as eating, bathing, dressing, and house-work. All services must be medically necessary.

Hospice

Hospice care is provided for patients who are termi-nally ill and have opted not to seek curative care. The focus is on comfort, not curing an illness. Drugs to make you more comfortable, counseling and medi-cally necessary supplies are covered. Most hospice services are provided in the home.

Medicare Part A will cover hospice care if your hos-pice doctor and regular doctor certify that you are terminally ill and have a life expectancy of six months or less. You must sign a statement saying that you are accepting palliative care instead of treatment for your illness.

Your hospice medical team must arrange for any ser-vices outside of palliative care, including short-term in-patient care, medications other than for symptoms or pain relief, visits to other physicians for conditions not related to your terminal illness, and emergency care.

Hospice care can be extended past six months with recertification from your physicians.

Worth Noting: Once you qualify for Social Security, you are eligible for Medicare at age 65.

Chapter 3

Part B

If you are eligible for Part A, you are eligible for Part B. If you are eligible for Social Security, you will be enrolled in both Part A and Part B automatically when you reach age 65.

Part B covers most doctor visits, lab tests, X-rays, outpatient procedures, and emergency room visits. It may cover medically necessary equipment and supplies such as canes, walkers, oxygen, and scooters.

Medicare does not cover dental, vision, or hearing aid services.

It is suggested you get approval from Medicare before purchasing any supplies or equipment. Everything must be deemed medically necessary for your specific condition. On Medicare's website, www.medicare.gov, you can enter the service or item in question and receive the conditions for which it will be covered by Medicare.

Part B is optional and you can reject it. If you do not accept Part B at the initial enrollment period, and sign up later, you will incur a permanent penalty. The premiums for Part B will be deducted from your monthly Social Security payment.

The standard Part B premium will be $134 in 2017, or higher depending on your past income. The deductible is increasing from $166 per year in 2016 to $183 in 2017.

The premium amounts will vary depending on your circumstances. The Hold Harmless Provision says that your Medicare Part B premium cannot be raised more than the Cost of Living Adjustment (COLA), which increases Social Security payments. In 2017, the COLA will raise Social Security payments between $4 and $5. Those whose payments for Part B coverage were deducted from their Social Security payment starting in 2015 or prior will pay $109 this year. Those who began having their Part B payments deducted in 2016 will pay $125. Others who earn less than $85,000 per year, will pay $134.

2017 Monthly Premium Amounts for Part B

- $109 – If you had your Medicare premium deducted from your Social Security payment starting in 2015 or prior.

- $125 – If you began having your Medicare premium deducted from your Social Security payment in 2016.

- $134 – All those who do not have a Medicare premium deducted from their Social Security payment now and earn less than $85,000 per year.

If your modified adjusted gross income reported to the IRS over the last two years was $85,000 or more, your premium payment will be higher.

For individuals:

- $85,000 to $107,000   Pays $187.50
- $107,000 to $160,000   Pays $267.90
- $160,000 to $214,000   Pays $348.30
- Above $214,000   Pays $428.60

For couples, each individual pays:

- $170,000 or less   Pays $134
- $170,000 to $214,000   Pays $187.50
- $214,000 to $320,000   Pays $267.90
- $320,000 to $428,000   Pays $348.30
- Above $428,000   Pays $428.60

Part B services are generally covered at 80% with the patient being responsible for the remaining 20%. This applies to services provided by doctors who participate in Medicare. For services with non-participating physicians, you may have to pay more. Find out if your doctor participates before receiving services so that you know what your responsibility will be.

Part B covers certain preventative procedures such as but not limited to colorectal screening, bone density testing, cancer screening, diabetes screening, glaucoma tests, HIV tests, flu shots, and a yearly wellness visit.

Unlike private insurance companies, which have a limit to how much you personally pay, there is no such limit with Medicare. There is no out-of-pocket maximum. Frequent doctor visits and laboratory testing can result in high costs to the patient.

For Part B:

- You must have Part A.

- Deductible is $183 per year.

- Premium is between $109 and $428.60 per month.

- Covers doctor visits, lab tests, X-rays, and more.

- Co-insurance is generally 20% of the cost of services.

Chapter 4

Part C

Part C, also known as Medicare Advantage Plans, are all-inclusive plans offered by private insurance companies. They operate like an HMO or PPO and offer a network of physicians and services in a specific area. Advantage Plans include Part A, Part B, and usually prescription drug coverage (Part D). You pay a premium for Part C in addition to your Part B premium.

You are eligible to enroll in a Part C plan if:

- You are eligible for Part A

- You are enrolled in Part B

- You live in the service area of the plan

Medicare Advantage Plans have the same coverage as Medicare Part A and Part B and usually offer additional benefits as well. Different companies offer different policies. Medicare Advantage Plans operate within a network of physicians and services. Most require you to have services by specific physicians at specific facilities, except in an emergency.

The rules and the premiums can change yearly. Different plans can charge different co-pays. You must review the plans available to you and make sure they provide the services that you need.

You can enroll in a Medicare Advantage Plan when you first sign up for Medicare or during the enrollment period from October 15 to December 7 each year.

The main attraction of the Medicare Advantage Plan is having the convenience of all of your services provided by one company with a network of interacting physicians that supervise your care, often under one roof. Your medical records are available to the different physicians as needed. It's the one-stop shopping of Medicare coverage.

You cannot be enrolled in both Medigap and a Medicare Advantage Plan. You have to have one or the other.

Chapter 5

Part D

Prescription Drug Coverage

- Medicare Part D is Prescription Drug Coverage.

- To qualify, you must participate in Part A and Part B.

- Medicare itself does not offer Part D policies. The coverage is provided by Medicare-approved insurance companies.

- Each company has the right to set prices, premiums, deductibles, co-pays, and decide which medications they cover.

- The policies must conform to certain standards, but the coverage can vary widely.

Medicare provides a Plan Finder on its website that will assist you in finding a company in your area that covers the medications you need. You enter your prescription name, dosage, and frequency. You will then get a list of companies and the cost of the premium, deductible, and co-pay required.

Insurance companies pay 75% of standard medications like those for blood pressure, heart disease and other common ailments. Once you reach a certain monetary level, you, the patient, are required to pay a higher percentage. This is known as the donut hole.

The idea of the donut hole is to have seniors pay part of the cost of their medications to decrease overspending and overutilization of prescription drugs. It would give retirees an incentive to use less expensive generic drugs and shop for better prices. It also prevents drug companies from being able to charge astronomical prices that seniors couldn't afford, but that Medicare would have to pay. Beware the *gap* or infamous *donut hole* in Part D policies outlined here:

- Once you and your insurance company have paid a combined amount of $3,700 for covered drugs during 2017, you enter the donut hole and the percentage of your coverage decreases. What you now pay increases.

- Once in the donut hole, your coverage decreases but you will pay no more than 40% of the cost of brand name prescriptions and 51% on generic drugs until you reach an out-of-pocket amount of $4,950. This will get you out of the gap or donut hole.

- Once you reach $4,950, you enter the cata- strophic coverage phase. Here the amount you pay goes down to a small percentage, about 6% – or about a $6.60 copay – for your prescriptions.

The percentage you pay for both brand name and generic drugs while in the donut hole is slowly de- creasing. It will go down to 25% in 2020. While some applaud this measure, others see it as an open door to wasteful spending.

The cost of Part D will vary depending on your past income and how much coverage you decide to pur- chase. There are plans as low as $12 per month and as high as $300 per month. Shop wisely.

Medicare does not cover dental, vision, or hearing aid services.

Chapter 6

Medigap

Medicare Supplemental Insurance

Medigap is also known as Medicare Supplemental Insurance. It is extra health insurance you buy from a private company that provides coverage for deductibles, co-pays, and services that are not covered by Medicare.

It fills the *Gap,* or the expenses Medicare does not cover.

Claims are first submitted to Medicare Part A and Part B. Any unpaid portion is then submitted to your Medigap company, which will cover all or part of the remaining charges. There is a premium for Medigap in addition to your Part B premium. The average is about $150 per month.

Medigap can only be provided by Medicare-approved companies. The policies are standardized. There are 10 types of Medigap Plans. Each plan provides a different range of coverage.

Medigap plans are standardized and offer the same coverage nationwide. The coverage for Plan A in New York will be the same as the coverage for Plan A in Colorado. Though the coverage is the same, the price can vary widely. It is important to shop for the best price available in your area and make sure you are not paying more for the exact same coverage.

Not all insurance companies provide each of the different plans, but they must offer Plan A, C, and F, if they offer any.

Massachusetts, Minnesota, and Wisconsin do not necessarily adhere to the standardized policies.

This 2017 chart is taken from the Medigap section of the Medicare website www.medicare.gov.

Medigap Benefits	A	B	C	D	F[∞]	G	K	L	M	N
Part A coinsurance and hospital costs up to an additional 365 days after Medicare benefits are used up	Yes	Yes	Yes	Yes	Yes	Yes	Yes	Yes	Yes	Yes
Part B coinsurance or copayment	Yes	Yes	Yes	Yes	Yes	Yes	50%	75%	Yes	Yes
Blood (first 3 pints)	Yes	Yes	Yes	Yes	Yes	Yes	50%	75%	Yes	Yes
Part A hospice care coinsurance or copayment	Yes	Yes	Yes	Yes	Yes	Yes	50%	75%	Yes	Yes
Skilled nursing facility care coinsurance	No	No	Yes	Yes	Yes	Yes	50%	75%	Yes	Yes
Part A deductible	No	Yes	Yes	Yes	Yes	Yes	50%	75%	50%	Yes
Part B deductible	No	No	Yes	No	Yes	No	No	No	No	No
Part B (excess charge)	No	No	No	No	Yes	Yes	No	No	No	No
Foreign travel exchange (up to plan limits)	No	No	80%	80%	80%	80%	No	No	80%	80%

Yes = the plan covers 100% of this benefit, No = the policy doesn't cover it % = the plan covers that percentage of this benefit. N/A = not applicable

The cost of a Medigap policy is about $150 per month. The initial cost of a policy may or may not be age dependent. Premiums may or may not be able to increase with time. Check your policy carefully.

Medigap or Supplemental Insurance:

- Is in addition to Part A and Part B coverage.

- May pay for premiums, deductibles, non-covered services and co-pays.

- Has 10 standardized policies lettered A–N

- Prices vary but average about $150 per month.

- Does not cover spouses. Each individual must have his/her own policy.

Conclusion

Medicare is the national health insurance plan for workers in the United States age 65 or older. It was founded in 1965 at a time when older and disabled American's found it impossible to get medical coverage. Medicare provides health care when we become disabled or aged. Many recipients no longer work and are not covered by insurance provided by an employer.

Having Medicare coverage is a blessing. It has improved the health and wellbeing of millions of our citizens and families. It has increased the quality of life of the entire nation.

Let's hope that we have the benefit of Medicare for many generations to come.

References

Social Security

Full Retirement Age

http://www.ssa.gov/retire2/retirechart.htm

https://www.nasi.org/learn/socialsecurity/
retirement-age

Social Security Retirement Planner

http://www.ssa.gov/planners/

Contributions to the Economy

http://www.aarp.org/content/dam/aarp/research/
public_policy_institute/econ_sec/2013/social-se-
curity-impact-national-economy-AARP-ppi-econ-sec.
pdf

Undocumented Workers

http://www.politifact.com/punditfact/state-
ments/2016/oct/02/maria-teresa-kumar/
how-much-do-undocumented-immigrants-pay-taxes/

https://news.vice.com/article/unauthorized-immigrants-paid-100-billion-into-social-security-over-last-decade

Railroad Retirement Program

www.ssa.gov/policy/docs/ssb/v68n2/v68n2p41.html

Benefit Estimator

http://www.socialsecurity.gov/retire2/estimator.htm

Bipartisan Budget Act of 2015

https://www.socialsecurity.gov/legislation/Bipartisan%20Budget%20Act%20Closes%20Social%20Security%20Loophole.pdf

Longevity

http://stgist.com/2016/12/11/cdc-life-expectancy-in-america-down-for-the-first-time-in-23-years/

http://www.lifehealthpro.com/2016/05/27/9-factors-that-affect-longevity?slreturn=1482588193&page=9

Windfall Elimination Provision

http://www.socialsecurity.gov/pubs/EN-05-10045.pdf

Government Pension Offset

http://www.socialsecurity.gov/retire2/gpo.htm

Spousal Benefits

http://www.socialsecurity.gov/retire2/applying6.htm

Benefits for the Divorced

https://www.ssa.gov/planners/retire/divspouse.html

http://www.wiserwomen.org/index.php%-3Fid%3D219%26page%3DSocial_Security_and_Divorce:_What_You_Need_to_Know

http://www.aarp.org/work/social-security/info-2016/divorced-social-security-benefits.html

Same-Sex Couples

https://www.socialsecurity.gov/people/same-sex-couples/

https://faq.ssa.gov/link/portal/34011/34019/ArticleFolder/452/Same-Sex-Couples

http://www.forbes.com/sites/nextavenue/2015/09/15/the-new-social-security-rules-for-same-sex-couples/#58d3c7982f40

Survivors Benefits

www.socialsecurity.gov/pubs/EN-05-10084.pdf

Online Office Locator

https://secure.ssa.gov/ICON/main.jsp#officeResults

Living Abroad

https://www.ssa.gov/international/payments_outsi-deUS.html

https://thunfinancial.com/social-security-ameri-can-expats-retirement-abroad/

https://www.ssa.gov/pubs/EN-05-10137.pdf

http://www.elderlawanswers.com/getting-social-se-curity-while-living-overseas-8301

Medicare

Medicare and You 2016

https://www.medicare.gov/medicare-and-you/medicare-and-you.html

Costs at a Glance 2015 and 2016

https://www.medicare.gov/your-medicare-costs/costs-at-a-glance/costs-at-glance.html

Part A

http://www.medicare.gov/what-medicare-covers/part-a/what-part-a-covers.html

Part B

http://www.medicare.gov/what-medicare-covers/part-b/what-medicare-part-b-covers.html

Part C

http://www.medicare.gov/sign-up-change-plans/
medicare-health-plans/medicare-advantage-plans/
medicare-advantage-plans.html

Medigap

http://www.medicare.gov/supplement-other-insur-
ance/medigap/whats-medigap.html

Plan A-N

https://www.medicare.gov/supplement-other-insur-
ance/compare-medigap/compare-medigap.html

Companies approved by Medicare

http://www.medicare.gov/find-a-plan/questions/
medigap-home.aspx

Part D

http://www.medicare.gov/part-d/

Medicare Plan Finder

http://www.medicare.gov/sign-up-change-plans/
get-drug-coverage/get-drug-coverage.html

Acknowledgements

This book was written with the support and encouragement of so many people. A special thank you goes to my dear friend, Judy Hill Lovins, whose unwavering support keeps me going. Thank you to her husband, Amory Lovins, for letting me take up so much of her time.

Many thanks to Marcia Dick, whose experience and editing skill was invaluable in getting this book published. You helped me through it.

Stefanie Kilts—I could not have done this without you. Thank you for amiably sticking with me through the many challenges. Your advice and dedication have been incomparable. I appreciate your knowledge and skill in marketing and social media. You've definitely taken this book to the next level and beyond.

Cathi Stevenson, thank you for the outstanding cover design and all the accessory pieces that go along with it. I appreciate your talent, your professionalism, and your timeliness. No sooner do I ask for something and voila, there it is. I'm very fortunate to have you in my corner.

DJ Rogers, thank you for taking my pile of pages and turning it into a beautiful book. I will always be grateful.

Shanti, my furry friend, who relentlessly insists I get up every few hours and go for a walk. Without her, my health, appearance, and spirit would deteriorate rapidly.

I offer my sincere gratitude to all of my friends and family that have helped make this book a reality and for their help in bringing insight to baby boomers across the land.

Om Shanti, peace to all.

About the Author

DONNA DAVIS, DC is a doctor of chiropractic, certified health coach, massage therapist, writer and author of the bestselling book, *The New Retirement Basics: The Quick and Easy Guide for Social Security and Medicare* 2016 and *Retirement Basics: Help for Broke Baby Boomers*. She is also a featured writer for the online magazine *Sixty and Me*, where she informs readers on how to have a happier, healthier and more secure future during retirement. Graduating New York Chiropractic College with an award in Meritorious Service, Dr. Davis grew up in New York City where she operated her private practice for 14 years. Since 1997, she has worked in the ski industry in Aspen Colorado, in which capacity she has twice been awarded the "Business Partner of the Year" award from *Habitat for Humanity*, in recognition of her innovative and charitable work for the community. A baby boomer approaching retirement herself, Dr. Davis has created *"Boomer Blasts"*, a website dedicated to helping retirees deal with the sometimes overwhelming challenges that come as a part of aging, especially in the areas of finances and health. Now living in Snowmass Village, Colorado, she is a passionate skier, hiker, traveler and animal lover.

Made in the USA
San Bernardino, CA
23 April 2018